THE UNENDING CONFLICT

Hilaire Belloc

Comprising

THE CHURCH & SOCIALISM
1908

BECKET
1933

WORLD CONFLICT
1951

CATHOLIC TRUTH SOCIETY

PUBLISHERS TO THE HOLY SEE

From the vantage-point of the Catholic attitude the meaningless pattern of the world falls into perspective…The Faith explains; it explains fully; and it is the only thing that does explain.

Historian, poet, novelist and political theorist, Belloc (1871-1953) was for most Englishmen the definition of a Catholic writer.

CTS ONEFIFTIES

The Church & Socialism originally published 1908; *Becket*, 1933
(reprinted from *The English Way: Studies in English Sanctity*,
Sheed & Ward, 1933); *World Conflict*, 1951.
Published by The Incorporated Catholic Truth Society,
40-46 Harleyford Road, London SE11 5AY
www.ctsbooks.org
All rights reserved.
Copyright © 2017 The Incorporated Catholic Truth Society.
ISBN 978 1 78469 528 6

THE CHURCH AND SOCIALISM

Hilaire Belloc

THE CHURCH AND SOCIALISM

HILAIRE BELLOC

The Catholic Church is throughout the world opposed to that modern theory of society which is called *Socialist*, the full and most logical form of which is Communism.

That is a plain fact which both parties to the quarrel recognize and which third parties, though they commonly explain it ill, recognize also.

It is further evident that, the nearer the Socialist theory comes to its moment of experiment, the larger the number of souls over which it obtains possession, the more definite and the more uncompromising does Catholic opposition to it become. But this native opposition between the Faith and Socialism is not one out of many phenomena connected with Socialism. It is the chief.

The movement of Socialism, as it advances, discovers no other serious opponent besides the Catholic Church; and in a general survey of Europe I cannot but believe that the struggle between these two forces is the matter of our immediate future.

The arguments which Socialists are accustomed to meet in their own non-Catholic surroundings are either puerile or vicious; the demolition of such arguments is too facile a task to occupy an intelligent mind, and the Socialist by the very exercise of such a controversy against ineptitude grows to think there is no permanent obstacle to the propagation of his system. He comes to think that his success is merely a question of time. Give him time to illuminate the darkened and to let it be exactly known what he desires, and all—or at least the vast unfortunate mass which make up the bulk and stuff of our modern industrial society—must agree with him.

In such a mood of ultimate intellectual security the Socialist comes across the Catholic Church and for the first time meets a barrier. He finds opposed to him an organism whose principle of life is opposed to his own, and an intelligence whose reasoning does not—as do the vulgar capitalist arguments to which he is so dreadfully accustomed—take for granted the very postulates of his own creed. He learns, the more he comes across this Catholic opposition, that he cannot lay to avarice, stupidity, or hypocrisy the resistance which this, to him, unfamiliar organism offers to his propaganda. Even in this country, where less is known of the Catholic Church than in any other, he has an example. The Irish people deliberately chose to be peasant proprietors upon terms most onerous and delayed, when they could immediately and on far more advantageous terms have become permanent tenants of the State. Such a political attitude in a whole people arrests a Socialist. He cannot lay it to the avarice of the rich: it was on the contrary, the act of men who were then among the poorest in western Christendom. He cannot lay it to the moral influence of a wealthy class indoctrinating the rest of the community with the idea of property, for of all the nations of Europe the Irish are the least subject to oligarchy. He cannot but observe that a people completely democratic and occupied in redressing the most glaring example of the evil which he, the Socialist, combats, have determined to redress it upon the lines of private ownership and not of collectivism. The concentration of the means of production in few hands, the exploitation of the whole community by a few, had reached in Ireland, after three hundred years of anti-Catholic administration, the very limits of human endurance. It was the worst case in Europe and the very field, a Socialist would think, for the immediate acceptance of collectivism; and yet private ownership, with its complexity, its perils and its anxieties, was deliberately chosen instead.

Again, the Socialist can but notice when he first comes across them that the Catholic priesthood and the men and women incorporated as Catholic Religious are the most resolute in their opposition to his campaign; and yet these are the only institutions in Europe to which poverty is, as it were, native: they are the only institutions which revive under poverty and are at their best and healthiest when they are least able to enjoy wealth; and, what is more, they are the only flourishing institutions in which the means of production are often held in a corporate manner.

There remains one facile explanation which, for a moment, the Socialist may accept. The Catholic resistance he may for a moment, when he first meets it, ascribe to stupidity. He may believe, as was universally believed in Oxford in my time (and, since that place is isolated, is probably still believed there), that no intelligent and trained man sincerely holds the Faith, and that a true conviction of it is possible only to those in whom ignorance or lack of exercise have atrophied the powers of reason. I say the Socialist may imagine this for a moment, in his first shock of surprise at finding men so fixedly opposed to his conceptions, but his very activity in propaganda will soon change such a judgment. Real Socialists and especially avowed Communists are at once the most sincere and the most actively curious of men. They seek out everywhere men of all kinds in order to convince them of justice: it is their occupation and their very breath; and in this process they will learn what all travelled and experienced men appreciate, that the spirit of the Church is not a spirit of intellectual supineness. The Catholic irony, the Catholic rhetoric, the Catholic rapidity of synthesis, the Catholic predilection for general ideas and for strict deduction therefrom, the Catholic passion for definition and precise thought—all these may spring from one erroneous attitude towards the Universe; but whatever that attitude is, most certainly (says the man with a wide experience of European life) it is not an attitude inimical to the exercise of thought. The Church breeds a continual vivacity of intellectual effort, which is discoverable both in history and in contemporary experience. It is alive with an intellectual activity which is perpetually supporting and extending a firm scheme of general philosophy, and is perpetually applying it to the concrete and ever-changing details of society. Those countries which have preserved Catholic tradition may be and are blamed by their opponents for too great an attachment to abstract principles and to ideas: not for the opposite tendency which shirks the effort of thinking and codifying and takes refuge in mere experiment.

The Socialist, then, who comes at all frequently upon Catholic opposition to his creed, grows interested in that opposition as in something novel and challenging to him. After so many unworthy opponents he inclines to look at the Catholic view of economic society as an orthodox Victorian economist, tired of answering idiotic objections to Free Trade, might look at a society hitherto unknown to him and actually advancing to prosperity through Protection. To put it in few words, Catholic opposition always, nearly always, makes a Socialist *think*. He recognizes that he has before him another world, another order of ideas from those which he has taken for granted in his opponents as in himself.

Two societies and two vast organisms meet in this quarrel. The one will necessarily, and that in the near future, attempt to destroy the other; they cannot co-exist; it is of supreme importance to all of us to-day to grasp the nature of the division.

What is it in Catholicism which negatives the Socialist's solution? Here is modern industrial society, evil beyond expression, cruel, unjust, cowardly and horribly insecure. The Socialist comes forward with an obvious and simple remedy. Let private property in land and the means of production be abolished, and let the State control them: let all become workmen under the State, which shall have absolute economic control over the lives of all and preserve to all security and sufficiency. Why does the Church, to which this modern industrial society is loathsome, and which is combating it with all her might; why does the Church, which continually points to the abominations of our great cities as a proof of what men come to by abandoning her; why does the Church, whose every doctrine is offended and denied by this evil, reject the solution offered? It is because she perceives in a certain proportion and order the exercise of human faculties; and having grasped that arrangement she refuses to sacrifice the greater to the lesser, the primary to the secondary thing: she will not imperil what is fundamental in society for the sake of some accidental need, nor deny what is permanent for the convenience of passing conditions. In all the miseries and shipwrecks of the sexual relation she will not admit one exception to the institution of marriage. In all the corruption and injustice of political society she will not abandon the principle of a social order with its necessary authorities, subordinations, and sanctions.

And to-day in all the disease of economic society and amid all the horrors which the abuse of property has brought about, she will not deny the institution of property, which she discovers to be normal to man—a condition of his freedom in civic action, but much more a necessity of his being.

I will put my argument upon a purely temporal basis for the simple reason that upon any other basis it is not an argument at all. One cannot argue with a man save upon common premisses; and since those to whom this explanation is addressed would never admit the premiss of revelation or of Divine knowledge in the Church, no appeal can be made to it if one desires to explain to them what it is that the Church rejects in their attitude.

Put, then, in purely temporal terms, the Church is a supreme expert in men. Not only is she an expert in the nature of men, but she is from the necessity of her constitution, experience, and expectation of the future, an institution which only considers men in the absolute. The Church will never give a definition that shall apply to men under particular and ephemeral conditions alone, nor, conversely, will she ever accept as general or true a definition constructed only for peculiar and ephemeral conditions. She is concerned with man for ever, and is here to preserve, even in mortal conditions, permanent and enduring things. For instance, to a man of the twelfth century resident in any agricultural part of Northern and Western Europe it would have seemed the most monstrous of absurdities and the most wicked of doctrines that a man should not be under a lord; the whole of society was permeated with that idea, yet the Church did not at that time define the feudal relation. She continued to lay down only what is universally true, saying in most universal terms that if civil society is to exist, subordination to constituted authority was a prime condition; and secondly that such subordination must repose upon a moral basis and had no sanction in mere force. The function of authority, whether in the commander or the commanded, was superior to both.

Now the Catholic Church, as an expert in men and as an expert whose peculiar character it is to refuse as general anything which does not cover the whole nature of man, rejects in Socialism its particular economic thesis—which is its distinguishing mark—but much more rejects, I mean more instinctively and with a more profound reaction, the consequences and connotations of that thesis.

The fundamental thesis of Socialism is this—that man would be better and happier were the means of production in human society, that is, land and machinery and all transport, controlled by Government rather than by private persons or corporations. If the Socialist regards that as universally true, then he holds what may justly be called a Socialist creed, he holds a general theory true under all conditions and at all times; and that creed the Catholic Church rejects. She maintains (I am not speaking here of her Divine authority or of her claim to speak with the voice of Divine revelation, but only of her judgment upon the nature of men)—she maintains, I say, that human society is fulfilling the end of its being, is normal to itself, is therefore happier, when its constituent families own and privately control material things; and she further maintains (just what, as we have seen, she did in the matter of civil authority) that this institution of ownership is not merely a civil accident unconnected with the destiny of the soul, nor a thing deliberately set up by man as are so many of the institutions of a State but a prior thing, connected with the nature of man, inseparable from him, and close in touch with the sense of right and wrong. Ownership for a Catholic involves definite moral obligations, exterior to and superior to ownership, but the right of ownership remains. The owner may be a very bad man, the thing owned may be of very little use to him and of great use to another; it still remains *his*, and the evil of depriving him of it is an evil wrought against what the Church regards as a fundamental human conception without which humanity cannot repose nor enjoy the sense of justice satisfied.

Let no Socialist say at this point that so absolute a proposition as that which I have called the fundamental Socialist thesis is not his; that some part of property in the means of production he will always admit: still less let him, in meeting a Catholic, indulge in a hoary fallacy and argue from the necessary influence of the State in economic affairs that Socialism is but an extension of an admitted principle. Every Catholic, from the nature of his creed, is possessed of the elements of philosophy, and every Catholic perceives that to the very existence of a system some definable principle is necessary. The principle of Socialism is that the means of production are morally the property not of individuals but of the State; that in the hands of individuals, however widely diffused, such property exploits the labour of others, and that such exploitation is wrong. No exceptions in practice destroy the validity of such a proposition; it is the prime conception which makes a Socialist what he is. The men who hold this doctrine fast, who see it clearly, and who attempt to act upon it and to convert others to it, are the true Socialists. They are numerous, and what is more, they are the core of the whole Socialist movement. It is their uncompromising dogma which gives it its vitality; for never could so vast a revolution be effected in human habit as Socialists in general pretend to effect, were there not ready to act for it men possessed of a definite and absolute creed.

For example, let us ask Socialists what they think of a

community composed of, we will say, two farming families. The one family owns a dairy farm of pasture; the other owns a farm mainly arable. The two farms are of approximately equal value. Each family is the owner of its farm and each employs the members of the other in certain forms of labour at certain seasons. The pasture farm hires labour from the arable farm at haytime, and the arable farm from the pasture farm at harvest. To the Catholic such a condition of society presents itself as absolutely just. Here is at once ownership, a fundamental human necessity; and yet no inequality, still less any grievance based upon the contrast between luxury above and want below.

Now, your true Socialist rejects a society of that kind. He says that even if the exact balance were struck, and even if the two owning families here supposed had precisely equal enjoyment of material things (a condition which, note you, the Socialist does not propose, for it is not equality of enjoyment that he is seeking, but the Socialisation of the means of production, which he regards as morally exterior to the category of ownable things), even then he would disapprove of such a community; for though each member of it was exploiting the other equally, yet *exploitation was going on*, and exploitation of itself he conceives to be morally wrong. Note that it is this fundamental attitude which makes the Socialist more bitter against schemes for the dispersion of capital than he is against schemes for its accumulation in few hands. Capital held by many—still more capital held by all, each with a share that forbids him to be proletarian in the State—is the opposite and the contradiction of the Socialist ideal. It is, on the contrary, the consummation of the Catholic ideal; and it is curious to note how those of the chief nations of Europe which resisted the "Reformation" have, since that crisis, tended to the perpetual accumulation of small capital in many hands, while societies which succumbed to the storm have tended to the accumulation of capital in few hands, and to the turning of the mass of citizens into a proletariat economically unfree. Contrast Protestant and Catholic cantons of Switzerland, France and Ireland with England, North Germany with South, etc., and this general historical truth will—with many exceptions—be apparent.

The whole of this quarrel may be put in a nutshell thus: The Catholic Church does not admit that the possession of the means of production is immoral as distinct from the possession of objects which cannot be used or are not used as means of production.

Now there arises on this point a very interesting question, which a man not a Socialist, but convinced that a temporary Socialist experiment is necessary if society is to be saved, may put with great force. All rules with regard to the nature of man are subject, says he, to the existence at least of mankind: and all lesser rights, however fundamental, must give way before the supreme right of the citizen to live. For instance, shipwrecked sailors upon a raft at sea may justly declare all food common property. The Catholic Church, with its doctrine of a certain minimum below which society may not compel a man to live, with its profound contempt for the results of wealth upon individual character, and with its acute perception of the order or ratio in which men supply their needs, is the first to perceive the necessity for exceptions to many of her own rules. And the questioner I am supposing may say to her this: "Since as a fact our society has got into this abnormally wicked condition in which a handful own the means of production and the mass are economically their slaves, will you not regard it as an exceptional time, and, under circumstances so abnormal and so vicious, promote the establishment, for a time at least, of the

Socialist principle?" This was the position which a Protestant of course and a member of the Ministry at the time (the late Mr. Masterman) took up in a debate at the New Reform Club some time ago. He said: Try collectivism, and of course it will turn into divided ownership; but you must have collectivism as a preliminary step.

To this question the Catholic Church again replies in the negative, and her reason for so replying is as follows: That the time in which we live, though historically considered it is most abnormal and vicious in its economical arrangements—perhaps in modern England worse than ever any society was before*—yet is not fatally bound to these arrangements. Those arrangements are not inevitable things which humanity must suffer; they are not due to external or natural forces which man is not responsible for: they are the direct results of a false philosophy and a vicious training of the mind. The Catholic Church replies to those who point out the monstrous inequalities into which industrial society has allowed itself to drift, that such inequalities have arisen through a myriad tiny agencies all of which have their root in the same false philosophy of life which is now attempting to remedy its own errors by the introduction of a remedy still reposing on the same false philosophy: the remedy of Socialism. It was precisely because men wanted to enjoy rather than to own, because they lost the sense of what is fundamental in man, that they promoted a machinery by which first the great landlord of the "Reformation" rising on the ruins of religion was economically dominant, next the merchant capitalist reached the head of affairs, until now more and more the mere gambler or the mere swindler enjoys supreme economic power in our diseased and moribund economic

---
* These words were written long before the Socialist experiment in the Russian towns.

society. It was precisely because the old European sense of personal connection between the owner and the thing owned was repudiated and lost when the true conception of human life was repudiated and lost with the loss of the Faith, that these monstrous financial fortunes which are the very negation of property at last arose. And the Catholic Church can reply to those who oppose her in this matter, that though she rejects the short cut of Socialism, society can still remedy itself, slowly indeed but effectually, by the adoption of her system with its full consequences, conscious and subconscious, upon every human action and upon the framing of laws. She would further reply that the adoption of but one principle of hers, the sanctity of property, and its consequent diffusion with the corresponding suspicion and repression of all forms of acquisition which depend less upon production than upon violence or intrigue, would transform society. It is a remedy which every politician could apply who desired to see free men freely possessed as citizens of the means of production, which every voter if he were in earnest could apply, which every writer if he were in earnest could apply.

The Catholic Church, acutely conscious as she is of the abominations of the modern industrial and capitalistic system, sees that system to be dependent upon human wills and curable by their right ordering. She refuses to cure it at the expense of denying a fundamental principle of morality, the principle of private ownership, which applies quite as much to the means of production as to any other class of material objects.

I will not extend these remarks nor expand the slight scope of my paper by showing that the refusal of the Catholic Church to admit Socialism is not a merely negative, but rather a constructive attitude. Every Catholic knows instinctively, as it were, that the erection of society upon Catholic lines makes for the destruction of servitude in every form. Every Catholic knows that Catholic morality produced the European peasant out of the material of the Pagan slave, every Catholic knows that it is in Catholic societies that revolt against intolerable economic conditions has been most fruitful, and every Catholic further knows how impossible it would be and is to establish in a fully Catholic society the monstrous institution of industrial capitalism. In a word, a Catholic feels that a Catholic society dealing with modern methods of production would be a society admitting great differences in the properties possessed by and controlled by individuals, but that it would of its nature eliminate that type of citizen who is in possession of none of the means of production and is proletarian. The Catholic Church—I speak here continually of its historical and temporal action, not of its revealed doctrine—knows men so thoroughly that, while insisting upon equality in certain temporal rights and in all spiritual things, it does not insist upon equality in economic enjoyment, for the simple reason that what men primarily need in this province is not equality but sufficiency and security. The Catholic conscience is convinced that sufficiency and security are more permanently attached to a society of divided ownership with the responsibilities, the family organizations, the sense of inheritance, the mutual obligations which make it an organic and forbid it to be a mechanical thing, than they are attached to the deliberate action of a despotic government. Now, a Catholic, relying upon Catholic training in thought and morals, can go further. He can say that were you to attempt the establishment of Socialism your effort could not but ultimately result in some form, and that a very evil form, of private ownership, with the controllers fewer and more powerful than ever.

Personally I cannot but see the future in this light. A society in which the Church shall conquer will be a society in which a proletariat shall be as unthinkable as it was unthinkable in the Middle Ages. Such a society would, under modern conditions of production, end as a society of highly divided properties bound together by free co-operative organizations. On the other hand, a society in which one Socialist experiment after another takes its place in the scheme of laws will not end as the ideal collectivist society which those just, sincere, and ardent men whom I am here opposing propose. It is far more likely to end as a state in which a very small class of free owners shall control a very large servile class into which the mass of citizens shall have sunk.

This is the peril which I believe to lie before society, and especially before the non-Catholic societies of Northern and industrial Europe, with their subservience to finance and their inheritance of an anti-Catholic philosophy. Every step towards the artificial regulation of contract brings us nearer some such final solution; and a solution it will be, though I dread it. A society once established upon those lines would have forgotten how to rebel; the security and sufficiency of the servile class would be the price of their servility, and the sense of freedom, with its incalculable consequences on human character, will, for the bulk of our descendants, have disappeared. It is a peril inconceivable to either party in the great modern quarrel, but it is close at hand. The only alternative I can see to that peril is, even in the temporal and economic sphere, the action and effect of the Catholic Church upon citizenship.

P.S.—The above paper was written in 1909. In 1917, upon the collapse of Russian society under the strain of the Great War, certain conspirators having as their chief director a certain

Braunstein (who concealed himself under the false Russian name of Trotsky), established Socialism in the greater part of the Russian towns. At the time when this paper was first revised (1921) this system, maintained by a rigid military discipline, still survived there. It had the same director put up as a figure-head, one Lenin, a Russian who was connected with Braunstein's clique by his domestic relations. The lamentable condition of the Russian towns under this experiment, its reliance upon the worst forms of terror, its disgusting excesses, and its increasing failure even as an economic system have been the theme of innumerable exhortations, most of them designed to support the industrial system.

At the moment of the second and present revision of this paper, 1931, Lenin being dead, another figurehead, one Stalin has been set up and Braunstein set aside, but incidentally the same clique controls the experiment. It is making desperate efforts to establish itself permanently and still greater ones to spread communism in the west.

By far the chief moral to be drawn from the whole tragedy has been carefully avoided by the bulk of the Industrial Press in Europe, and has been wholly ignored in Britain. It is this: *The one barrier to the spread of Socialism (Communism) over Christendom from its Russian centres has been the Catholic Church.* A real or affected ignorance of this truth has warped half our foreign policy, and has, in particular, weakened our own future in Europe by a complete misunderstanding of the Polish people and their position as the bulwark of civilisation in the East.

BECKET

Hilaire Belloc

BECKET:
ST. THOMAS OF CANTERBURY

HILAIRE BELLOC

The life and death of Thomas à Becket, Archbishop of Canterbury, may be put in the phrase "Constancy and its Fruit." Now the fruit of constancy is not what the constant agent himself immediately desired. This is because man is a subordinate. He cannot fashion the future to his will; he is used by God.

Men are used. The purposes of God, which guide the universe, cannot be the purposes of one man. But if that one man's purpose is humble and direct, open and good (which means in unison with God's purpose), then he would rejoice at the fruit of his constancy. Though it should not be that which he had desired, it will be consonant with what he had desired. It will be found larger than what he had desired. It will be found more permanent than what he had desired. He will serve God in a sense unwittingly, though wittingly in purpose. But he will glorify God in the result.

Each man who has achieved, has achieved something other than he intended. Each man who has achieved, has achieved something in the same axis with, along the same direction, as his intention was—in proportion as his intention was good.

Reprinted, by permission, from *The English Way: Studies in English Sanctity from Bede to Newman.* (Sheed & Ward: Large Cr. 8vo., 328 pp., 7s. 6d. net.)

In the history of Western Europe the episode of the martyrdom at Canterbury is a capital example of constancy. It stands out the more vividly because, in that very place, in that very See, the purpose for which St. Thomas died has been conspicuously denied, ridiculed, frustrated, and (locally) destroyed.

The principle for which St. Thomas suffered martyrdom was this:

That the Church of God is a visible single universal society, with powers superior to those of this world, and therefore of right, *autonomous*. That principle is the negation of the opposite, of the base, ephemeral, thing already passing from Christian life, sometimes called pedantically "Erastianism"; the principle that the divine and permanent is subject to the human and passing power. St. Thomas died for the doctrine, the truth, that the link with eternal things must never be broken under the pressure of ephemeral desires, that the control of eternal things cannot, in morals, be subjected to the ephemeral arrangements of men.

But note this—that his constancy was exercised for a particular form in which that truth applied to the society of his own time. The specific detailed formula for which he laid down his life, later lost its meaning because in the perpetual flux of human arrangements words and conditions changed. The ultimate principle remained unchanged. He fought against an attempt of the civil power in his time to subject the Church of God to its jurisdiction in a particular fashion which since then has ceased to be of moment, and almost ceased to be of meaning. On which account it might be asked whether it were worth while for him to have fought at all. But he gained a victory for the essential principle, so that in his image one man after another arose (and shall in future arise) who have and will—God granting them grace—maintain that same principle: that the things of God are not subject to the judgment of men.

St. Thomas fought against what was in his time a certain innovation, but an innovation apparently so slight, certainly so subtle, and above all so convenient to the general spirit of the time, that it seemed—though an innovation—a piece of common sense which only an obdurate, fanatical man would resist: someone anchored in the past or wedded to a dead ancient formula. He fought against an innovation put forward in sixteen articles, called "The Constitutions of Clarendon"; of which sixteen articles many were tolerable enough, and all arguable, and every one of which in one form or another has lapsed from the area of conflict into that of agreed things. The two conspicuous points upon which he resisted were: (1) the judgment by the civil courts of clerics of whatever rank when first accused of a crime—a privilege still existing in Canon Law but in practice everywhere abolished, and (2) the rule that there should be no appeals in spiritual matters to the sovereign pontiff without leave of the king. On this second point the position has been turned by the fact that the non-Christian modern governments (whatever may be true of the future) do not recognise the Supreme Pontiff, nor indeed any such thing as a spiritual court. So our appeals may go forward merrily enough, only Cæsar does not admit any jurisdiction in the final court to which they are preferred—nor, as a rule, any matter for appeal. If I desire my marriage to be declared null I may appeal to Rome without leave of the state, because the state does not admit as yet in modern countries that Rome has jurisdiction in such affairs. And though Rome declare my marriage null I am, under Cæsar's modern law, bigamous if I marry again, or (what is much more probable) if Rome declares me bound to my wife, I am no adulterer in Cæsar's eyes if under Cæsar's law I marry another.

How then can it be true that St. Thomas—having apparently technically succeeded by his constancy upon two points which even in his own time seemed to many dubious, and these points having in practice become devoid of any practical meaning to-day—achieved, and that his constancy bore fruit? In this way. That his heroic resistance prevented the assault of the temporal power against the eternal from being fatal at the moment when, precisely, it might have been fatal.

To put it bluntly, he saved the Church. He came, he was raised up, he was murdered for God, just at the moment which might have been the turn of the tide towards secularisation. He checked it for four hundred years. The tide flowed on, but not to the complete destruction of Christian unity. The great intellectual and therefore sceptical movement of the twelfth century was prevented from disrupting Christendom; the tide flowed on, then slackened. The organisation of the Church grew old, the arteries of its human organisation hardened; by the end of the fifteenth century, more than 300 years after the killing of that man at Canterbury Cathedral, the time was ripe for a greater assault, and the assault was delivered. In part it conquered, but not *wholly*, as, but for St. Thomas, it might have done far earlier.

Fools or provincials would say that the last assault conquered altogether. It certainly has not done so. The extent of its conquest is still debatable. But had not St. Thomas died, even the occasion of this modern debate would not have arisen, for already, at the beginning of the great mediæval spring, the Church would have failed.

That, in saving the Church, he saved society itself, was instinctively felt by the common people, through whose spontaneous piety Almighty God achieves his purposes more widely than through any other channel, save perhaps through the channel of individual holiness and courage. The common people, not the clergy (though it was to their interest) in a burst of enthusiasm imposed the worship of the martyr upon Christendom. They felt it in their bones (and they were right) that if the laical state—the seeds of which were being sown—should once rise to maturity and complete power they would be what they have become to-day, half-way to slavery. The independence of the Church was the guarantee of their customs and of that spirit whereby Christian men grope towards, in part always enjoy, and necessarily and always proclaim, freedom. It required the imbecility of modern Dons to wonder why St. Thomas should have so suddenly become a popular saint—why Canterbury should have become one of the great shrines of Christendom—and to decide that it was due to some odd mechanical conspiracy on the part of the priests! It was one of the most unplanned things that ever happened in history. It rose like a spring out of the earth exactly as, in a quite different field of spiritual appeal, there sprang in our own day the recognition of St. Theresa of Lisieux: a young woman high among the Saints of God.

There is another major consideration in the matter of this great saint. Is it better to be direct or subtle? I mean, is it better for the purposes of God to be direct or subtle? Which is the better for one's own soul there can be no doubt. But is it better to be direct or subtle for the achievement of the Kingdom?

Now to that unending doubt there are, as to all unending doubts, two answers equally valid. For there are conditions under which to be subtle is essential, when, without subtlety, there is nothing but disaster, even in the matters of the soul;

and there are also conditions under which (and this is more easily forgotten by the tortuous and fallen spirit of man) for the achievement of the Kingdom it is better to be direct and to challenge.

Were not the first method admissible human affairs, and therefore the affairs of God on earth, would be a chaos and would fail. But for those who ridicule the second method as something impossible or, what is worse to the intelligence, grossly insufficient, St. Thomas provides an example. It happened to be his business, it happened to be his duty, it happened to be his triumph, to be direct. As against the multiple, to be single; as against the diverse, to be absolute; as against manœuvre, to charge.

There is yet another question arising from this great story. It is the most searching question of all. "What about pride?" All challengers suffer, of necessity, the temptation of pride. They are of the breed of certitude and of simplicity; being simple and certain they will brook no contradiction; they are as it were blindly convinced of the right—and the right is their right. Now to make certain that you are always right is to put yourself in the position of God, and in so far as you put yourself in the position of God you are suffering from the weakness and nastiness of pride. These protagonists have always been accused of that fatal flaw in themselves. What is much more important for the comprehension of their very selves, they have always been at least *tempted* to it: now a permanent temptation is part of character, but by the Grace of God it is not necessarily a mastering part.

It is true, then, that all the great protagonists have had pride for a companion. To yield to it is their temptation, but it is a constitutional tendency and not a motive of their energy.

They are sure. None shall deflect them. Yet their object being something outside themselves, they have in them a solvent of the evil thing; and I will believe that those who appear before the throne of God after heavy battles in the right cause, yet clouded with too much opinion, will have it easily forgiven them; especially if they have been defeated in the battles of the Lord.

Yet let this also be noted: that the instruments which are chosen for work of this kind, those of the Tertullian spirit, cannot but be of that human sort which is imperfect through aggression and assertiveness and edge. They are sent out to dig like chisels; they must of necessity offend on that against which they act; for every permanent work is done in hard material and against the grain. Were they not what they are, nothing would be achieved for the Kingdom—or, at least, all would be only half done.

If these things be so (and they are so) let us consider the process whereby this great saint came to his glory.

What we today call England, a certain unmistakable unit, a nation, was created by the success of the Bastard William of Falaise, called "The Conqueror," when he confirmed by arms his claim to rule the country. (The word "conquest" is deceptive. There was in his day no modern idea of the violent unjust rape of one territory by the people of another—but to discuss all that would take too long.) What we call England was made, grew from, began, upon a Sussex hill in 1066. Not that the blood which we call English began then and (God knows) not the landscape nor the deep things which inhabit the native soul. All these are immemorial; the English imagination, the English humour, the English Englishry is from the beginning of recorded time. The pirate invasions from the "Angulus" or Bight of Denmark, their few colonies on the eastern coast, never profoundly affected this island. Nor is language a guide. But just when Europe was turning to a crystallisation of nations out of that circling cauldron of the Dark Ages, England also was crystallised; and it was the Norman influence which precipitated her thus from a boiling into a crystallisation. The process had not gone on a lifetime when St. Thomas was born.

We do not know the exact date of his birth. It was almost certainly between fifty and fifty-five years after the decisive battle which put the Bastard of Normandy, William, upon the throne at Westminster. It is thought that the year 1118 may be the most probable guess. St. Thomas was born in London, in Cheapside, at the end of December, the son of a London merchant, who had begun business upon the other side of the channel in Rouen, and had there secured wealth. It was a time when, for now nearly a hundred years past, the directing classes of England had been more and more mixed with the Continent and in which they had more and more come to be French-speaking—as must have been St. Thomas himself and all his people. The distinction between the gentry and merchants had not re-arisen (it is the nature of society, and crops up period after period). His father was of gentle blood in the sense that the family had been territorial in Normandy, nor did St. Thomas ever feel himself to be other than the equal of those with whom he mixed. He was a huge powerful young man, good at every bodily exercise, a fighter on horseback; he certainly had ambition, and he was helped therein by those through whom he rose. He was of a world alive and eager, and when after his first advancements, partly perhaps through the wealth of his father, much through the recognition of his abilities, and more from the protection of the first man in the kingdom, the Archbishop of Canterbury, who promoted him, he rose. He took the Plantagenet side in the days when the young Plantagenet heir who was to be Henry II, at least ten years younger than himself, came by certain accidents to be the King of England. This Henry II of England sprang from the famous house of Anjou; packed with vitality, showing sparse red hair, intense, violent, exact; and the two men of similar energy became closely bound together.

Now this Henry II of England, this new king of the new Angevin stock, great-grandson of William the Conqueror, married the divorced wife of the King of France. She was the heiress of all the west and the south, and her young husband became not only King of England but, under a sort of feudal homage, real ruler beyond Normandy (which he had inherited on the English side), also of all the South and West of the French kingdom. He was thus in his active and battling youth possessed of a greater recruiting field and a greater revenue than the French King, his Sovereign; and upon his will the future of Europe would largely depend. Therefore St. Thomas as his bosom friend and fellow-in-arms stood out also before Christendom. Thomas fought for his junior, the king, during the expedition into Southern France in 1159, seven years after Henry's accession; he became glorious through a single combat with another man, saddle to saddle; he was the soldier of his day. His young master and friend determined to make him his all-sufficient minister, the title of such in that day being "Chancellor."* That young determined king of so much, and lord of half the West, did more for him. Henry being thirty years of age and St. Thomas about or over forty, the king determined

---

* The term, though preserved, has of course nothing in common with the modern title of Lord Chancellor, which applies to some chance lawyer or other who has worked his way through Parliament.

to make him Archbishop of Canterbury, and thereby to make him also the first man in the kingdom.

It is essential to understand what this meant. In theory the monks of Canterbury could elect their Archbishop; in practice for centuries, the king really nominated him.

The Church throughout the West was one body; the English province of the Church—or rather the two provinces of the Church in England, York and Canterbury—had been but part, for four hundred years at least, of Western Christendom. The unity of the Church had survived an anxious disruptive period after the death of Charlemagne more than three hundred years before, when, for the better part of two centuries, all manner of disturbances and quarrels had threatened to overwhelm Christendom. In that interlude—that interregnum as it were of our civilisation—all manner of disruptive forces threatened us. The Mahomedans who had swept over half Christendom perpetually attacked in the South; Mongol and Slav Pagans from the East; Scandinavians from the North; the great landowners made themselves masters over their districts, and there survived of the imperial authority almost nothing, of local royal authority very little. The revenues of the Church, fixed in ancient endowments of land, fell in part a prey to the great families. But the structure of society held fast; the Mass, all the Liturgy, the hierarchy, the framework—clerical and lay—stood.

About a hundred years before St. Thomas's birth the energies of Christendom began to raise a new dawn; and for that century those energies proceeded to a rapid extension of architecture and letters and learning. We have the vast adventure of the Crusades; we have the revivified powers of the Papacy, always admitted and always in the very nature of our society, but now to be fully exercised. With all this there went a new discipline throughout the Church; the enforcement of the long lapse in the matter of celibacy and an increasing clarity in the organisation which would bind Christendom together. But at the same time there came necessarily, with greater wealth and clearer thinking and more eager ambitions, the growth of power in the Princes—of whom Henry II of England was among the very first.

It was in such a conjuncture, with the power of the Pope now well and consciously organised, with all Christendom knowing that on it, and the full society of the Church in hierarchy below it, the future would depend—for that civilisation was at stake in a rising quarrel between the independent universal Church and the local magnates—it was just at such a crisis that "Thomas of London" as he signed himself, was, on the insistence of his companion-in-arms and deep friend, the younger man Henry, put into the See of Canterbury.

He was consecrated on Sunday, June 3rd, 1162, to the See which his old patron had occupied and which had been vacant for a year. It was a Sunday which St. Thomas in memory of the event turned into that Feast of the Trinity, the name of which has been preserved ever since. We must never forget that it was from Canterbury that the Feast of the Trinity proceeded, as did that other solemn Catholic custom, the Elevation of the Host after consecration at Mass.*

Immediately upon St. Thomas's elevation to the throne of Canterbury the inevitable clash between his strong character and the strong character of his junior, his close friend, his king

---

* Landfranc, St. Thomas's chief predecessor and first Archbishop of Canterbury in the new England, was the great defender of the Real Presence, when the first doubts began to be cast upon it in France during his youth, and in reparation, or by way of especial homage, he would hold the Host reverently in his hands after consecration, lifting it somewhat in front of his face, and it seems that it was from this gesture that the full Elevation developed.

appeared. For St. Thomas, authoritative, determined and always laying upon himself a clear course and always holding a clear definition both of his rights, but still more of his duty, was now the unquestioned head of the Church in England, and the Church was not a part of the State, was not indeed a *part* of Christendom; it was the *soul* of Christendom, superior to any local government and independent of any temporal government, not only in all that concerned doctrine but in all that concerned its own discipline and personnel.

With the awakening of a new and greater civilisation in this twelfth century and with the revival of the old doctrines of imperial right under the lay imperial code of the Roman Empire this superior, intangible, autonomous character of the Church was challenged. An effort could not but arise on the part of the lay power to make the Church within that power more and more subordinate to the earthly monarch of the realm. England, the best organised state of the time, and Henry its King, now lord of Normandy and all Western France as well, Henry, who was upon the whole the strongest monarch in Christendom, still young (little over thirty) and of a fiery energy, could not but move as he did. He began an attempted control over that part of the universal Church which lay within his frontiers. Had he at once and wholly succeeded the disaster, which was as a fact postponed for four hundred years, would have begun in the twelfth instead of the sixteenth century and—what is much more important than a mere postponement—it would have been universal, it would have affected the whole structure of the Church and condemned that structure to decay; it would not have been a mere division of Christendom, leaving a Catholic portion saved and sound, but a sapping of the vital principle of Christendom throughout Europe.

The moment for the revolutionary change proposed by this first Plantagenet was after a fashion inevitable, for it corresponded to another change which had come upon the Church itself. The main body of the Church officials, the "clerics," from its earliest days to the close of the dark ages, was composed of the hierarchy: priests and bishops. Less than the priests, but usually on their way to becoming priests, were the deacons and sub-deacons. There were also many who were in lesser orders and were still called "clerics," though not, properly speaking, of the sacred hierarchy. The general tone was given by the priest, he was the *typical* cleric; the lesser clerics were only a fringe. The determining number which gave its colour and tone to the mass of ecclesiastics, those who would be generally recognised under the term "clergy," were the fully qualified priests who alone could consecrate and offer up the sacrifice of the Mass. The great bulk of them were settled as parish priests, though there was also a large number who were unattached, candidates for endowment who had not yet received it and might never receive it.

Now at the end of the Dark Ages and the first stirrings of the high mediæval civilisation, that is, with those last years of the tenth century when it was clear that Europe had saved herself from barbarian and Mahomedan pressure and the great siege was at an end; when one reform after another, each more thorough than the last, was leading up through more than a lifetime of effort to the Cluniac movement and at last to the glorious achievement of St. Gregory VII, when the origins of the Crusades had appeared in Spain, when a new culture was beginning in the schools and an administration more and more developed in the local courts, the clerical members were vastly increased.

They were so increased *not* by the addition of a great number of new priests, but by a great number of new men whose activities were secular, though they were tonsured and affiliated to the clerical body. These kept the accounts, they studied and systematised the old and new laws, they were the writers, the negotiators and the calculators; they filled the growing mass of minor posts which the new civilisation had produced; they fulfilled nearly all the duties which could not be fulfilled either by the fighting class or by those who cultivated the soil, or by the artisans. It is from this great mass of non-priestly but clerical men that there has been derived our word "clerk," and in general the identification of the word "clerical" with the whole business of writing. Those who taught were clerics, most of those who negotiated between princes were clerics, those who looked after the papers of public or private wealth were clerics.

The consequence was that the State was now—by 1162—newly faced with the presence of a new vast clerical body, fulfilling the functions and liable to the temptations and accidents of the layman. It was newly faced with thousands of individuals who were technically part of the clerical—that is to say, the Church—organisation, and therefore amenable only to the Church law and the Church courts, and yet in daily avocation what today we should call laymen.

This state of affairs was not only the excuse, but in part the cause of the king's novel attempt: but he made no distinction between the various parts of the clerical body, and if his policy had won, any priest, however exalted his position, would have fallen (as he has fallen in modern times) under the lay power. The mediæval autonomy of the Church would have disappeared, and with it, soon, religion and the unity of Christendom.

In the first year after the new Archbishop had been enthroned the great quarrel broke out. At Woodstock, in that royal manor on the land which was later made over to Marlborough as a reward for Blenheim, the king published "The Constitutions of Clarendon." Here we must note very carefully what these were and—a very different thing—what they purported to be.

The document purported to be "a record or recognition" of his grandfather's (Henry I) *customs* in Church matters, the *accepted* Church law of the realm. It is of the first importance to mark that. There was no admitted innovation. Such an idea would have been abhorrent to the time. The only test of right was custom; and to effect this beginning of revolution a pretence had to be made that it was an old custom which was being claimed and which furnished the moral basis for the action which the king proposed to take. But the thing was a falsehood. Although the document includes in its sixteen clauses not a few customs which had indeed tradition behind them, it also contains two of the utmost moment, both of which were revolutionary. These two clauses were the third and the eighth, and it is interesting to note the subtlety with which those who served the king attempted to give to a novelty (and a subversive novelty at the time) an excuse.

The eighth clause lays it down that no ecclesiastical appeal could be carried beyond the king's court (that is, to Rome) without leave of the king. Appeal could be made from the archdeacon to the bishop, from the bishop to the archbishop, and from the archbishop to the king, but the further appeal to Rome was declared to be against custom and right save when it was especially permitted by the Crown. Observe here this question of the old custom and right, at any rate since the Conquest. The Crown had claimed, the Church had never admitted, the right to prevent *recorded pronouncements* passing into or out of the kingdom without the royal leave. Thus a Papal Bull could not be introduced into England after the Conquest save by leave of the king; but it had never been admitted, I say, as a moral right by the Church: it could not be so, for to admit it would be to make the unity of the Church dependent upon the will of a local sovereign. It had been a custom of force and not of agreement between the two separate powers. But this new eighth clause in the Constitutions of Clarendon said something quite different. It said that there was no constitutional right of appeal from English ecclesiastical courts to Rome; they laid it down that *custom* so deemed; and so to lay down the custom was a falsehood.

Much more important in practice (because in practice appeals would have constantly been allowed anyway) was the third clause of the sixteen, which was the one round which in reality all the battle was to rage. By this clause the personnel of the Church, the members of that international and supernational body coincident with the Papal authority and with all western Christendom, was to be treated—in this realm at least—as the laymen were treated, and to be regarded in the administration as subjects of the king, and not as officers of a universal church. Hitherto any cleric accused of a crime could be tried by his ecclesiastical superiors only. They could for a grave crime degrade him, were he to offend again he would then be tried of course as a layman, his privilege of clergy had gone. But the principle was clear and universal, that while he was still a cleric he was amenable to clerical jurisdiction alone.

The introduction of this capital revolution was effected, as I have said, with great subtlety of phrase. "Clerics accused in any matter" (it ran) "being summoned by the king's justice and the Ecclesiastical Court, it may be seen what matter should be replied to in that Court . . . . so that the king's justice shall send into the Court of Holy Church to see for what reason the matter is being dealt with there. And if the cleric be convicted or shall confess, he should not further be protected by the Church."

This is on the face of it much more tentative and much more of a compromise than we are usually told in our textbooks, where we are informed that the king proposed purely and simply to take jurisdiction out of the Church's hands. The form of words was such that a well-meaning ecclesiastical authority might be deceived and that men too timid to resist might salve their consciences.

It was clear that the intention was—it would at any rate soon be made the effect of such a clause—that clerics accused of a crime should in practice be withdrawn from ecclesiastical jurisdiction and treated as laymen. But it might be argued from the form of words that all that was going to happen was a courteous discussion between the lay and ecclesiastical power as to what the man was had up for, and whether it really did concern the Church, etc., etc. It is of capital importance to remember this in the story of what follows.

This document containing these revolutionary proposals, the Constitutions of Clarendon (it is a short thing, less than 2,000 words in length) is drawn up in the form in which it had been assented to by the magnates of the kingdom, including the bishops, and at the head of the list of those who assented was the name and title of Thomas, Archbishop of Canterbury, the first man in the realm and the head of the English province of the Church Universal. *The Constitutions were accepted*. The lay lords accepted them of course, but so did the bishops, and (possibly under a verbal misunderstanding) the Pope.

St. Thomas himself accepted them, but he had already grasped the core of the matter; he accepted grievously and with grave reluctance after a delay of three days, saying that he must obey the Pope, but that such obedience was compelling him to perjury—meaning presumably that he never could in practice agree to the changes proposed. All had begun in the summer of the year after St. Thomas's enthronement as Archbishop, in the month of July, 1163. In October a Council at Westminster confirmed the Constitutions. But the resistance of St. Thomas was beginning. When the bishops agreed, they had only agreed (presumably under St. Thomas's influence) with the clause added, "saving our order." The bishops in their turn had influenced St. Thomas in his agreement as late as January of the next year, 1164, when all the great of the realm were again summoned to Clarendon.

But St. Thomas believed that he had acted like St. Peter; his conscience would not let him rest, and Henry knew that it would soon be open war between them.

He saw the Archbishop twice, he understood what resistance he was to be prepared for, and he summoned for the October of that year (1164) another great council at Northampton. Instead of sending a special summons to the first man of the realm—the Archbishop and Primate—he sent for him by orders to the officers of the County of Kent, a planned belittling, and an insult to one whom he now regarded as an enemy.

St. Thomas came to that great meeting, and was there an isolated man. He appeared in the outer hall, with his huge figure standing out above them all, grasping his Cross in his own hand instead of having it borne before him, as though for a symbol that he alone, Thomas the individual soul, was standing out with none to befriend him or support him.

The bishops of England, some of whom were his personal enemies, but most of whom at heart knew that he was doing right, begged him to yield. He retorted by solemnly telling them that it was *their* duty to obey *his* authority.

The quarrel grew fiercer, Henry forbade an appeal to Rome, and told the council to denounce the saint for a traitor. The king's attitude was modified for a moment through the hesitation of the bishops, when they saw how grave the matter had become; he allowed the appeal to Rome, but he carried out a policy of violent financial persecution, demanding huge sums from the See of Canterbury upon various pleas of chicanery; and on All Souls' Day of that year (1164) St. Thomas secretly sailed from Sandwich to take refuge upon the Continent, to see the supreme Pontiff of Christendom in person and to be free from the peril of direct constraint. Before the end of November he had seen Pope Alexander III at Sens. He laid at the feet of the Papal authority two things; the text of the Constitutions against which he was holding out, and his archiepiscopal ring—the tender of which meant that he was willing, or rather anxious, to resign his See and so leave the decision to his successor, and the Pope free.

At this point we must particularly regard the attitude taken by Alexander III, the Pope of the day. It can be too much excused, but it can also be maligned.

Alexander III was one of the great political Popes who have, in the Providence of God, been preservative of Catholic political power in the world. He was engaged in a struggle against the greatest of the Emperors, Barbarossa, and was defending not only the liberties of Rome and the Church, but of the Italian cities. The Emperor and his Germans had set up against him an anti-Pope, and Alexander was at this moment in France because he was virtually exiled from Italy by the strength of his opponent. It was of the highest moment that so powerful a king as Henry should not join forces with the new German schism. Anyhow, whether he is to be praised upon the whole or blamed, the Pope, deliberately considering all the circumstances, chose to temporise. He would not allow St. Thomas to resign; he said that the Constitutions of Clarendon were not to be accepted as a whole, but that six of them were acceptable—"tolerable" was the word—that is, to be accepted if necessary. In general his support of St. Thomas was lukewarm. He aimed at a reconciliation, and what is more, it seems that he still thought the issue to be only a verbal one, a question of formulation, of interpretation. If that were so, he was wrong and St. Thomas was right; it was not a verbal matter but a matter of vital principle, as the event would certainly show if ever the proposed changes were accepted.

There followed for years a swaying struggle, in which at moments St. Thomas was nearly reconciled to Henry—on condition of course that he was not made to accept the obnoxious thing—in the course of which Henry nearly yielded twice, but also in the course of which there were moments of acute tension and almost of violence. Thus, when St. Thomas took refuge with the Cistercians at Pontigny, Henry threatened in revenge to expel all the Cistercians from England. Towards the end of those uncertain years of St. Thomas's exile Henry went so far as to have his young son crowned by St. Thomas's especial enemy, the Archbishop of York, Roger de Pont l'Eveque—although the Primate alone had the right to crown the kings or heirs of England. To meet the threats that were taking place against ecclesiastical property and the usurpations of his enemies in his absence St. Thomas began to issue excommunications. He had even threatened that if Henry did not amend before Candlemas of the year 1170 he would be put under an interdict. It was in the June of that year that Henry committed the blunder and the outrage of having his young son crowned by Roger of York, though not only St. Thomas but the Pope himself had forbidden such action. The king feared he had gone too far, and began to go back. A few weeks later, at Fréteval, he was so far reconciled that he promised to be guided by the Archbishop's counsel, and to keep silent upon the whole revolutionary policy of ecclesiastical jurisdiction. He even openly proposed to return to England in the company of St. Thomas. But he delayed, and made shifts for further delay, until at the end of the year, in the November of 1170, St. Thomas proceeded to the final actions which culminated in his martyrdom.

It was proposed to send the saint back to his See, the property of which was to be restored and the administration put again into his hands; but as a sort of warder over him during the journey was set John of Oxford, a notorious enemy with whom he would not have been safe, and he learnt that Roger of York and the Bishops of London and Salisbury, who were also especially opposed to him, were plotting to prevent his landing. St. Thomas had obtained from the Pope letters inhibiting and conditionally excommunicating those who opposed the Primate. He sent these letters across the Channel in advance of himself, dispatching them on Sunday, November 29, while he sailed on Monday, November 30, from Wyssant—the little port between Calais and Boulogne then often used—and on the next day, Tuesday, December 1, he landed at Sandwich and proceeded to his palace and cathedral at Canterbury. He there reiterated his position again fully and awaited whatever results might follow from his firmness. Those against whom he had moved the Pope to act demanded unconditional absolution. He replied that he must await the Pope's further letters. And they proceeded to the king in order to lodge their appeal. Meanwhile, the property of the See was not restored, as had been promised, and to the burning indignation of the Archbishop, the immediate lands of the archbishopric were in the hands of robbers and despoilers, notably a lawless brigand of a fellow, De Broc, who had seized one of the archiepiscopal castles, Saltwood, and was making it a nest of robbers.

On Friday, Christmas Day, St. Thomas excommunicated De Broc, and four days later—Tuesday, December 29—appeared those four knights who had acted upon the king's passionate words, and were ready to slay. They bade St. Thomas absolve the bishops. He was steadfast, and refused. It was the afternoon of that winter day, and the sun was already sinking, when they came back armed and with them De Broc, determined to save his booty and to that end to extract his own absolution by force. In the presence of these five men, now armed, the monks dragged their great master with them into the cathedral, through the cloisters by the north door. They would have barred the door, but St. Thomas forbade them to do so. The light was now failing and the great church was half in darkness when the armed murderers burst in by that north door. All fled save one Grim, who stood by his master, holding the Archbishop's Cross in his hand. The swords were drawn, and with one of them the Archbishop's cap was struck off. He knelt upon the stone floor of the North Transept, not far from the corner pillar thereof where one turned into the Ambulatory round the Choir. So kneeling he covered his face with his hands. He was no longer throwing back angrily into the teeth of his opponents the insults they had given him: he saw that death was upon him. And as he so knelt, with his hands before his face, he murmured, "To God and Blessed Mary, to the patron Saints of this Church and

St. Denis I commend myself and the cause of the Faith." He bowed his head and awaited the blow. The first that struck was Fitzurse; Grim put up his hand to shield his master, but his arm was broken and the sword gashed that master's head. Another blow followed, and he fell. A third cut off the crown of the skull and with the sword's point the brains were scattered upon the stones. Then, having done these things, they left the body where it lay and fled out into the now dark winter air.

Those few moments of tragedy in the North Transept of Canterbury had done what so many years of effort had so far failed to do. The whole movement against the autonomy of the Church was stopped dead. The tide ran rapidly backward—within an hour St. Thomas was a martyr, within a month the champion not only of religion but of the common people, who obscurely but firmly knew that the independence of the Church was their safeguard. A tale of miracles began, and within a year the name of St. Thomas of Canterbury was standing permanently above and throughout Christendom. Everywhere there were chapels and churches raised to his name, and then came the great uninterrupted pilgrimages to his shrine year after year, till it rivalled St. James of Compostella, becoming the second great centre in the West and loaded with gems and gold and endowment.

WORLD CONFLICT

Hilaire Belloc

WORLD CONFLICT

Hilaire Belloc

We find ourselves in a world where we know our own existence and where something which Aristotle called "Common Sense" makes us recognise the reality of existences outside our own. Further, we find in ourselves senses of right and wrong, pleasure and pain. When we set out to interpret ourselves and the universe about us—to find out the meaning of the affair—our own origins and nature and destiny—whether there be a conscious will behind the universe—whether that will is indifferent to us or not, and so on: when we begin *that* supreme inquiry, we are brought to a halt. The great questions, the only questions the answers to which really matter, remain unanswered. It is doctrine indeed that the human mind can, unaided by revelation, discover that God is, that He is omnipotent, one and personal. But it is not doctrine (and still less is it experience) that every human mind can of its unaided power achieve this feat; and it is quite certain that not one in a thousand attempts it. As for the nature and destiny of man, his possible immortality, his responsibility, his free-will, we are left without a clue.

Faced with the great unanswered questions, the tendency of men, after a first examination, is to proclaim them unanswerable. Of course, where men do not trouble to think, merely accepting what they have been told, they may answer conventionally one or another of these great questions; but the moment they begin to reason, their first, most natural, attitude is scepticism. They conclude thus:

"We know nothing of these things. Nothing can be proved upon them, and therefore it is futile to continue the search, and puerile and ignoble to pretend to have discovered an answer. The man who does so is either abandoning the use of his reason and blindly accepting that to which he has been accustomed by long repetition since childhood, or he is a hypocrite and liar, and perhaps the worst sort of hypocrite and liar—the man who lies to himself in order to feel at ease."

Now it so happens that there is a third point of view or attitude of the mind neither sceptical nor the mere product of habit and repetition, but working upon the following lines:

"I have discovered an absolute Authority upon earth; I have heard a Voice which speaks on these affairs in the unmistakable tone of combined integrity and knowledge. I have come upon a Personality whose commands are at once justified, salutary, and (as it were) a part of my own being, because they proceed from that which was the Author of my being, to whom I tend and with whom I, like all creation, am in organic connection. The answers given by this Authority to the great unanswered questions, I accept as final and true."

This third attitude, which is neither the high sceptical attitude nor the confused "circular" attitude of mere habit, is called Catholic. It is the attitude which I who am writing these lines adopt in common with a good many other people. I adopt it with all its consequences in political and social action, in the general frame of the mind, in the texture of character which it produces, and in the duties which it imposes apart from, and sometimes in contradiction to, all lesser authorities whatsoever.

This third type of philosophy is unique. One hears men talk of "warring creeds," "conflicting systems" and "various religions," and including the Catholic Church in that general description as though it were of the same stuff as the rest. Such a confusion argues an ignorance of the matter discussed. Catholicism is not one opinion amongst many, nor one set of doctrines and customs amongst many others. It is of an essence different from all else. It is the only institution on earth which has ever proclaimed, and still does proclaim, itself infallible and absolutely authoritative. No one of those other institutions which seem to be of its own kind and nature (because they make many statements in common with Catholic statements or because they have a traditional ritual and body of doctrine largely in common with Catholicism—for instance, the Eastern Church) is really of the same stuff at all. For *they* say that there is no visible, localised, concrete, definite, citable authority of the kind. They admit no living and teaching authority amongst men to be continuously infallible and active to-day and for the future.

At the best they say there *has* been one in the past and *may* be one in the future. But the attitude of those who say that there *is* one, fully alive, and that it always has been and always will be such an authority, is peculiar to Catholics: that is (since one has to define accurately in these days of loose phraseology), peculiar to those who are in communion with the Papacy, accept the infallibility of its decisions and of the General Councils, not only in the past but as they are continued under authority to our own day.

There are certain strange marks to be observed attaching to this institution called "The Catholic Church." In the first place, while making this awful and unique and (in the eyes of most people) incredible claim to certitude based on reason (while no one else has certitude other than blind), it answers some questions only, others not at all. One might imagine that a system of the kind would pretend to universal knowledge; it professes none save on its own field. For instance, it affirms a creation. Our lesser, very interesting, questions upon the *mode* of creation it leaves unanswered. Next, note that it is and has been throughout the ages intensely loved, and even more intensely hated. The violence of that hatred is inconceivable to those who have not felt it. It arises only on contact. It is hardly felt in the absence of the irritant. But in the presence of that irritant hate blazes out like a fire.

Lastly, though hated, it is quite astonishingly unknown. It almost looks as though hardly any man not within this institution could possess the faculties whereby its character may be appreciated.

I have known one or two exceptions (perhaps half a dozen in my whole life) of men born and brought up outside the Catholic Church, never dreaming of accepting it as other than an illusion and man-made, yet really knowing what it was all about and of what stuff it was. These men were men of very wide reading in many languages and of wide travel and experience. But to one such there are a hundred equally well-read and equally widely travelled who are as much in error upon the savour and character of the Catholic Church as, say, the average French journalist is in error upon the nature of an English public school.

For instance, you will find men highly educated, and with a good knowledge of other things, who imagine that Catholicism in some way restricts intellectual exercise. They say this to *us*, to *us* who feel that our intelligence cannot act freely in any other atmosphere, who enjoy the whole range of human thought and the only complete philosophy! They tell us we are restricted from doing that which the Catholic alone has fully done for two thousand years, that is, looking into everything to find its cause, and searching continually for further and further detail in the general body of truth. Or again, they will regard Catholicism as a bundle of disconnected affirmations, some picturesque, some absurd, some obvious. They may live all their lives reading the history of a Catholic country, or period, and yet remain completely ignorant of the simple fact that the Faith is not only one vast coherent system, explanatory of the universe and of man therein, but a system which is so alive that it ramifies perpetually into a wider and wider exercise of faculty and meets and deals with every new situation with which it is confronted.

Again, you will find many people of fair instruction and fairly wide reading who imagine that Catholicism refuses to face reality, and organises this illusion, whereas the whole point of Catholicism is the facing of reality and the refusal to be drugged by mere repeated affirmation, or to do anything but laugh at the silly modern systems of self-deception which have arisen from a desire to avoid the ordeal of human life.

It is this character in the Faith—that it is universal, that it has the very ring of reality, that its authoritative voice is recognised at once if it be heard—it is this character, I say, which has brought into its orbit, as by an irresistible pressure, the best brains of our time. Among all other kinds of men it has been particularly those men who had the keener senses combined with the highest intelligence who have harked back to the religion of Europe. What that appeal of Catholicism to the intelligence may be I can perhaps best illustrate by a metaphor which I have always found singularly applicable.

The old painters often amused themselves by drawing a picture which at first sight looked like an unintelligible chaos. Put your eye in a particular position, and the picture falls at once into perspective and corresponds with that which it was meant to portray. There is such a detail in the National Gallery; among the objects appearing in a particular picture is one object which at first sight looks like nothing on earth: a long drawn, oval, yellowish thing with meaningless lights and darks upon it. Look at it from a particular point to the side of the picture and you will see it to be a skull; change your position slightly, and it resolves itself into chaos again. Now the Catholic attitude is like that. From the vantage-point of the Catholic attitude the meaningless pattern of the world falls into perspective. Catholic philosophy and action is found consonant with the life of man and with man's normal relation to the world about him. The Faith explains; it explains fully; and it is the only thing that does explain.

Nevertheless, as I have said, it is hated and suffers from a really astonishing ignorance of its character and habits in the minds of onlookers. On this account I suggest that conflict between the Catholic Church and the other forces of the modern world is imminent. Whether we have yet heard the first clash or no is debatable. Whether a recognised and violent open battle will be waged a short time hence or not till after a lifetime or more, no one can tell. But it is coming.

That which is not Catholic in the modern world is not only tending towards, it is racing towards, a new set of laws, a new condition of the civic mind which is incompatible with Catholicism. There cannot but be an atmosphere created in which, in the long run, either Catholicism will not be able to live, or its opponents will not be able to live.

There are many avenues by which we may see that state of things approaching. Perhaps the most important is that of the debate on Free Will (for all political questions are ultimately theological).

The Catholic Church may be called an Exercise of the Will. But as the modern world loses its remnants of Christian doctrine, the function of the Will not only declines, but is in prospect of being denied. The substitution of physical science for philosophy; of the quantitative for the qualitative; of unimportant things, directly demonstrable to the poorest mind, for important things which the greater minds grasp by appreciation—all this process is making for a clash between those who retain the doctrine of Free Will and those who have sunk unintelligently into the drift of materialism and fatalism; a conception that all the process of the world and of ourselves is inevitable. To take but one instance of an issue on which the clash might soon come; this new paganism tends to regard evil as due to impersonal causes. It tends to eliminate moral indignation and to deprive of its meaning the distinction between right and wrong.

Again, the denial of Free Will ultimately tends to restrict more and more the liberty of the individual. It tends indirectly, but with its whole power, to the sacrifice of human dignity for the purposes of a supposed collective temporal and merely material good. Here again the new paganism cannot but clash with the Catholic Church. We may be upon the edge of new laws which will enforce a declaration from parents to promote the sterilisation of the unfit. We may live to see new laws enforcing one system of general education to the exclusion of dogmatic teaching in schools under public authority, to which the mass of people are forced to send their children.

But particular instances give no idea of the magnitude of the quarrel. A whole social tissue is being built up as an organism about us, and the more coherent it becomes, the more its new personality is emphasised, the more violent and emphatic is its necessary quarrel with that opposing institution whereby alone, as I conceive, can man fulfil his being. For in the Catholic Church alone can man fulfil his being, or achieve such poor happiness as freedom and responsibility breed in this brief preparatory life between birth and death.

BACKGROUND

The Church and Socialism dates originally from 1908, when Belloc was Liberal MP for Salford (where Herbert Vaughan, CTS's founder, had been bishop before going to Westminster). It was revised in 1921, and again in 1931. It is a robust and eloquent defence of private property against collectivist solutions. *Becket* (1933) takes the familiar story of the martyred Archbishop of Canterbury, and explains its wider significance: how the Church resists the state's efforts to abridge her authority. *World Conflict* was first published in 1951, two years before Belloc's death; it was his last published work. It may stand as a colophon to his life's work, at least as a historian: to place before the reader, with all the forcible eloquence of which he was an unparalleled master, the reality of the Church as the only truly sane and wholesome way of making sense of the world and all its joys and sorrows.

CTS ONEFIFTIES

1. FR DAMIEN & WHERE ALL ROADS LEAD · *Robert Louis Stevenson & G K Chesterton*
2. THE UNENDING CONFLICT · *Hilaire Belloc*
3. CHRIST UPON THE WATERS · *John Henry Newman*
4. DEATH & RESURRECTION · *Leonard Cheshire VC & Bede Jarrett OP*
5. THE DAY THE BOMB FELL · *Johannes Siemes SJ & Bruce Kent*
6. MIRACLES · *Ronald Knox*
7. A CITY SET ON A HILL · *Robert Hugh Benson*
8. FINDING THE WAY BACK · *Francis Ripley*
9. THE GUNPOWDER PLOT · *Herbert Thurston SJ*
10. NUNS – WHAT ARE THEY FOR? · *Maria Boulding OSB, Bruno Webb OSB & Jean Cardinal Daniélou SJ*
11. ISLAM, BRITAIN & THE GOSPEL · *John Coonan, William Burridge & John Wijngaards*
12. STORIES OF THE GREAT WAR · *Eileen Boland*
13. LIFE WITHIN US · *Caryll Houselander, Delia Smith & Herbert Fincham*
14. INSIDE COMMUNISM · *Douglas Hyde*
15. COURTSHIP: SOME PRACTICAL ADVICE · *Anon, Hubert McEvoy SJ, Tony Kirwin & Malcolm Brennan*
16. RESURRECTION · *Vincent McNabb OP & B C Butler OSB*
17. TWO CONVERSION STORIES · *James Britten & Ronald Knox*
18. MEDIEVAL CHRISTIANITY · *Christopher Dawson*
19. A LIBRARY OF TALES – VOL 1 · *Lady Herbert of Lea*
20. A LIBRARY OF TALES – VOL 2 · *Eveline Cole & E Kielty*
21. WAR AT HOME AND AT THE FRONT · *"A Chaplain" & Mrs Blundell of Crosby*
22. THE CHURCH & THE MODERN AGE · *Christopher Hollis*
23. THE PRAYER OF ST THÉRÈSE OF LISIEUX · *Vernon Johnson*
24. THE PROBLEM OF EVIL · *Martin D'Arcy SJ*
25. WHO IS ST JOSEPH? · *Herbert Cardinal Vaughan*